SECRETS OF ANCIENT CIVILIZATIONS

I0867775

THE SECRET LIVES OF PHARAOHS

by Carol Kim

CAPSTONE PRESS
a capstone imprint

Published by Capstone Press, an imprint of Capstone
1710 Roe Crest Drive, North Mankato, Minnesota 56003
capstonepub.com

Copyright © 2025 by Capstone. All rights reserved. No part of this publication may be reproduced in whole or in part, or stored in a retrieval system, or transmitted in any form or by any means, electronic, mechanical, photocopying, recording, or otherwise, without written permission of the publisher.

Library of Congress Cataloging-in-Publication Data
is available on the Library of Congress website.
ISBN: 9781669087786 (hardcover)
ISBN: 9781669087908 (paperback)
ISBN: 9781669087748 (ebook PDF)

Summary: Pharaohs ruled ancient Egypt for 3,000 years. They may be gone, but their contributions remain for experts to discover and learn from. Modern science is finding answers to questions about their lives and challenging what historians thought they already knew. Learn more about the pharaohs and how modern science has helped reveal some of their secrets.

Editorial Credits
Editor: Mari Bolte; Designer: Bobbie Nuytten; Media Researcher: Svetlana Zhurkin; Production Specialist: Whitney Schaefer

Image Credits
Alamy: Michael DeFreitas Middle East, 28, North Wind Picture Archives, 10, 23; Bridgeman Images: © NPL–DeA Picture Library/W. Buss, 11; Getty Images: AFP/Cris Bouroncle, 27, Ibrahim Hamroush, 17, Margalliver, 22, Reed Kaestner, 7, ZU_09, 15; The Metropolitan Museum of Art: Rogers Fund, 1929, 21; Newscom: Danita Delimont Photography/ Kenneth Garrett, 25, Prisma/Album, 13; Shutterstock: Alejo Bernal (hieroglyphs), cover and throughout, art of line, 5, Cendrillon481, 6, Claudio Caridi, 19, Dunhill, 24, Jaroslav Moravcik, cover, 30, Kokhanchikov, 12, Mia Stendal (light rays), cover and throughout, Paolo Gallo, 8, Punnawit Suwattananun, 9, Ravenash, 14, Sailingstone Travel, 20, Sergii Figurnyi, 29, Vladimir Wrangel, 26; SuperStock: Mary Evans Picture Library, 18

Any additional websites and resources referenced in this book are not maintained, authorized, or sponsored by Capstone. All product and company names are trademarks™ or registered® trademarks of their respective holders.

Printed and bound in China. PO 6098

TABLE OF CONTENTS

Words in **bold** are in the glossary.

Introduction

FINDING THE LOST CITY

Egyptian archaeologist Zahi Hawass never stopped thinking about his next project. Every dig could give him the exciting chance to learn more about ancient Egypt and its leaders.

In September 2020, Hawass began a new search. His team hoped to find a worship site used by an ancient king named Tutankhamen. Only a few weeks into the dig, the crew began to uncover mud bricks. The bricks branched off in all directions. Soon, they realized they were unearthing a whole city.

The 3,000-year-old "Lost Golden City of Luxor" had been built under the rule of Amenhotep III. Hawass's team had been looking for a Tutankhamen **monument**. Instead, they found something built by his grandfather. It was the largest ancient Egyptian city ever discovered. The things buried inside provided fresh lessons about how Egypt was ruled.

Only a small portion of the Lost Golden City has been uncovered.

Chapter 1

LEADERS IN LIFE AND DEATH

Few civilizations lasted as long as ancient Egypt. It thrived for more than 3,000 years. Powerful leaders were called pharaohs. They shaped and controlled how the nation was run. Many succeeded in making Egypt wealthy and strong. Living in this thriving society allowed Egyptians to make advances in mathematics. They also valued language and the arts.

The Abu Simbel Temples were built by Ramses II, a New Kingdom pharaoh.

Around 30 different **dynasties** ruled from the beginning to the end of ancient Egypt. Each dynasty had different beliefs and priorities that shaped history. Scholars divide ancient Egypt's history into three periods. They are known as the Old, Middle, and New Kingdoms.

FACT

The lives of pharaohs were recorded with **hieroglyphs** that cover the walls of temples and tombs. Written documents about the daily lives of ancient Egyptians were recorded on **papyrus**.

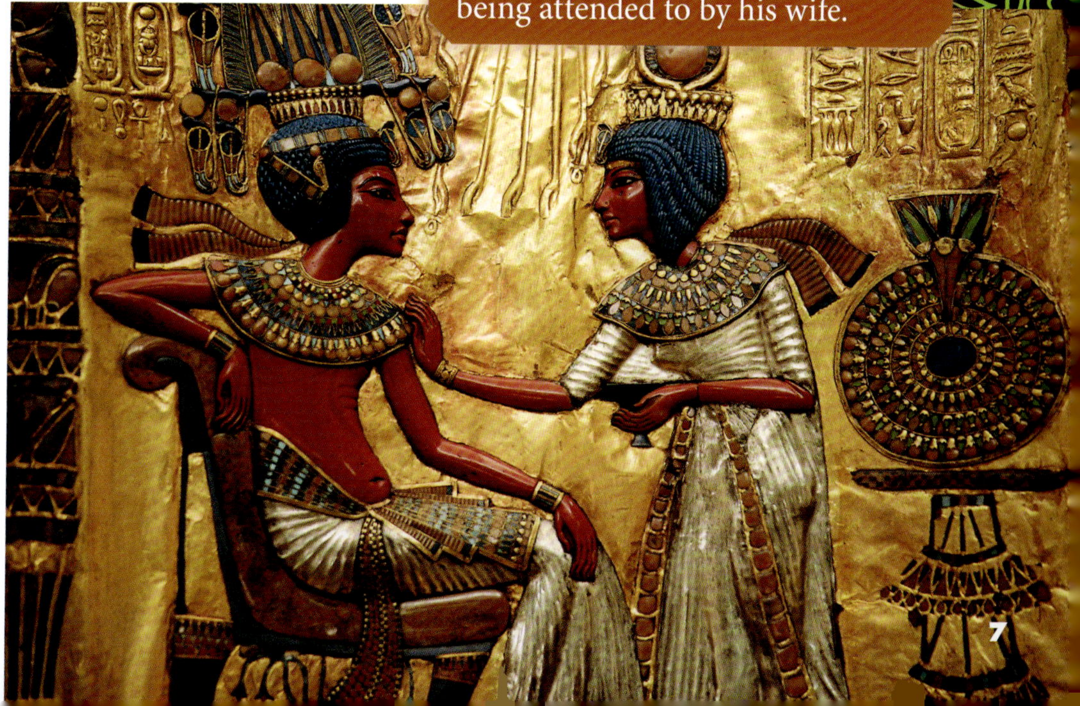

Tutankhamen's throne is decorated with art showing the young king being attended to by his wife.

Ancient Egyptians believed in the **afterlife**. Their bodies died. Their spiritual bodies would live on in a place very similar to the living world. Spells written on coffins and papyrus would help them arrive safely.

FACT

Early Egyptian rulers were called kings. The word pharaoh was not commonly used until the New Kingdom.

New Kingdom pharaohs were buried with the Book of the Dead. This ancient text included spells and formulas to protect the ruler in the afterlife.

When pharaohs died, they were buried in special tombs, such as pyramids or underground chambers. These tombs held the pharaoh's mummified body and many of their belongings. It took many years to build a pyramid. Some took 20 years or longer.

They were also expensive projects. Pharaohs needed to start while they were still alive. Much of what is known about their lives comes from studying these structures and the objects found inside.

The first pyramid was the Pyramid of Djoser. At least 117 others were built after that.

Chapter 2

A POWERFUL RESPONSIBILITY

The title of pharaoh was usually passed down from father to son. However, there were also female rulers. Sobekneferu, Hatshepsut, and Cleopatra were three women who ruled Egypt. Pharaohs often married a close relative. This kept the royal bloodline pure.

Experts disagree on the number of female pharaohs. Some think there were six. Others think there were a dozen—or more!

The pharaohs of ancient Egypt held unlimited power. Pharaohs made the laws, went to war, and set taxes. Egypt was often under threat. Drought and **famine** happened regularly. It often led to starvation and unrest.

Pharaohs' lives were ruled by their many responsibilities. Someone was with them every moment of the day. They had little time to themselves. There were also few people pharaohs could trust. Some were **assassinated** by those close to them.

The Best Job Title Ever

Attendants to the pharaoh held important positions. They also had fancy titles. An attendant who helped the king with his morning routine was the Chief of the Scented Oils and Pastes for Rubbing His Majesty's Body.

Fragrant oils were only affordable for the richest people in Egypt.

Religion was very important to ancient Egyptians. They built temples to honor more than 2,000 gods and goddesses. Myths and legends were recorded. Those stories were saved for today's experts to discover.

The pharaoh held the role of high priest. Each ruler was a link between regular people and the gods. In life, they spoke for Horus, the god of the sky. After death, pharaohs were connected to Osiris, the god of the underworld.

Horus was usually shown as a man with the head of a falcon.

Worshipping the gods was only one part of ancient leadership. The need for balance and order was also key. The word for this order was *ma'at*. As rulers and religious leaders, maintaining ma'at was the pharaoh's biggest responsibility.

Heb-Sed Festival

A celebration called Heb-Sed marked a pharaoh's 30th year of rule. Offerings were made and the king was re-crowned. At the end, the pharaoh dressed in a short kilt with a tail. Then, they ran around a track four times. This was to prove they were still fit enough to perform their duties as ruler. Another Heb-Sed was held every three years after that.

A scene from a pharaoh's Heb-Sed festival

Chapter 3

ROYAL LIFE

The life of a pharaoh was full of comfort and luxury. Pharaohs lived in huge palaces with many rooms. Each pharaoh built their own palaces. Rooms were decorated from floor to ceiling. However, the palaces were made of mud bricks. Most did not last into the modern day.

Tombs contained paintings and carvings. Ancient Egyptians believed that the images would travel to the afterlife with the dead.

Pharaohs had many people to take care of their every need. Bathing and grooming the pharaoh was a big responsibility. Workers rubbed the pharaoh's skin with oils and scents. Food was carefully prepared.

After being washed and dressed, the pharaoh would perform their official duties. During some periods in ancient history, pharaohs were seen as living gods and were treated as such. Only special people could meet with the king.

Tutankhamen holding an audience with an important official overseeing one of Egypt's territories

Pharaohs were busy. They took time to enjoy themselves, though. They held banquets and served huge amounts of food. The menu included meat, which most regular Egyptians hardly ever got to eat. There would also be entertainment with music and dancing.

Pharaohs enjoyed hunting and playing sports. There are many drawings showing pharaohs hunting hippopotamuses, elephants, and lions. There are descriptions of pharaohs swimming and riding in boats. Written accounts show that archery was a favorite pastime of Amenhotep, Tutankhamen, and Ramses II.

Pharaohs also enjoyed quieter activities. Several board games were found in Tutankhamen's tomb. Drawings of Queen Nefertari playing board games have been uncovered.

Queen Nefertari enjoyed playing a board game called senet.

Chapter 4

TAKING A CLOSER LOOK

The first king of ancient Egypt was Narmer. He is also known as Menes. He joined upper and lower Egypt around 3100 BCE. For another 3,000 years, ancient Egypt flourished. Around 170 pharaohs ruled Egypt during three separate periods.

Some experts believe that Narmer was the king's actual name, and Menes was an honorable title.

Old Kingdom (2686 to 2160 BCE)

The Old Kingdom is known as the age of the pyramids. Djoser (2630–2611 BCE) built the first step pyramid. He also saved Egypt from a seven-year famine. Researchers see Djoser as proof that pharaohs took care of their subjects' well-being.

Khufu (2609–2584 BCE) built the Great Pyramid of Giza. Early scientists believed that enslaved people built the huge structure. But later research of the builders' graves revealed that workers were free people. They were well cared for and had plenty of food.

The only surviving statue of Khufu is just 3 inches (7.5 centimeters) tall.

Middle Kingdom (2034 to 1650 BCE)

During the Middle Kingdom, the power of pharaohs began to weaken. Pharaohs were no longer seen as human gods. They were workers for the people. However, it was also a time of literature and art. The royal families began building huge monuments to the gods. Sobekneferu, also known as Neferusobek, ruled from 1807 to 1802 BCE. She was Egypt's first female leader and the last ruler of her dynasty.

Senusret I was another Middle Kingdom pharaoh. The White Chapel of Senusret I was built for his Heb-Sed festival.

New Kingdom (1550 to 1069 BCE)

Pharaohs of the New Kingdom were rich and powerful. They included Thutmose III, Amenhotep III, and Ramses II. Akhenaten and his son, Tutankhamen, were part of the New Kingdom as well.

One New Kingdom **regent**, Queen Hatshepsut (1478–1458 BCE) shared the throne with her stepson, Thutmose III. But later, in a bold move, she declared herself pharaoh. She ruled for 22 years. Her successful trading expeditions boosted her popularity. She built a grand temple and huge stone pillars. These structures reminded Egyptians of her wealth and power.

Nearly Forgotten

After Hatshepsut's death, Thutmose III tried to erase proof that she served as king. He ordered her image removed from monuments. He destroyed her statues. For centuries, her reign was forgotten. But 19th-century archaeologists found her tomb and restored her place in history.

Hatshepsut's history was lost until 1822, when hieroglyphics that told her story were discovered.

Ramses II (1279–1213 BCE) ruled Egypt for 66 years. He built many structures and statues bragging of his skill in battle. He was a legendary figure. For years, modern scholars called him Ramses the Great. But researchers have since found that Ramses II often exaggerated his successes. His death also marked the beginning of the end of the Egyptian empire.

Some of the greatest monuments in Egypt, including Luxor Temple, were worked on by Ramses II.

The Last Pharaoh

Cleopatra VII (51–30 BCE) ruled Egypt for 21 years alongside her brothers. She wanted to protect Egypt from being conquered. To do so, she forged relationships with Roman leaders Julius Caesar and Marc Antony. However, Antony was defeated by his rivals. Egypt fell to Rome. Cleopatra was the last pharaoh of Egypt.

Cleopatra and Antony's romance is one of the most well-known tragedies in history.

Chapter 5

CONTINUING EXPLORATION

Studying the pharaohs helps historians understand how ancient Egypt was so successful. With each passing year, new discoveries are being made.

One of the worst droughts in Egypt happened around 1250 to 1100 BCE. Scientists studied ancient pollen records and the DNA of cattle. The records showed that leaders took steps to prepare for the crisis. They grew and stored extra grain. They bred cattle that could survive the heat.

Oxen helped ancient Egyptians plow fields and water crops.

Modern **CT scans** are helping researchers solve some old mysteries about pharaohs' deaths. The scans reveal details that couldn't be seen using regular **X-rays**.

The pharaoh Seqenenre (1558–1555 BCE) died during a war with a foreign kingdom called Hyksos. However, some experts wondered if he had been assassinated. CT scans matched his wounds to weapons made in Hyksos. This proved he was killed during battle.

A scan of Ramses III (1186–1155 BCE) showed multiple fatal injuries sustained at the same time. This confirmed a theory that he had been killed as part of an assassination plot.

Zahi Hawass (left) oversees a CT scan of a mummy.

The missing tombs of Queen Nefertiti and Cleopatra have stumped archaeologists for a long time. Modern science may help them solve these mysteries.

Archaeologist Nicholas Reeves believes Nefertiti is buried in a hidden chamber within King Tutankhamen's tomb. Zahi Hawass believes her tomb will be found near the newly discovered Lost Golden City of Luxor.

Nefertiti's bust was found in a workshop in the city of Tell el-Amarna in Egypt.

Cleopatra was part of the Greek Ptolemaic Dynasty (305–30 BCE). None of the tombs belonging to the 14 Ptolemy pharaohs have been found. However, most **Egyptologists** believe they are buried in the ancient city of Alexandria. In August 2022, archaeologist Kathleen Martinez discovered a long tunnel 43 feet (13 meters) under the ground. Two years later, she shared the news that coins with Cleopatra's name and face had also been found inside.

FACT

Today, Alexandria is at the bottom of the Mediterranean Sea.

Kathleen Martinez has been looking for Cleopatra since 2004.

Conclusion

A NEVER-ENDING STORY

The pharaohs of Egypt survived many hardships. They dealt with wars and drought. They fought famine and threats from other countries and rulers. Even with these challenges, ancient Egypt remained one of the most successful and long-lasting civilizations in history.

Artifacts help anyone learn about life in ancient Egypt.

Archaeologists continue to search for and study everything they can about the pharaohs. These ancient rulers lived thousands of years ago. However, they continue to teach us valuable lessons that are still useful today.

Many of the leaders can inspire us. Some built huge monuments. Others showed that women can be just as successful as men. They embraced the arts and the written word. Both were tools that would allow their successes and contributions to be discovered and studied centuries later.

Although they were built thousands of years ago, monuments such as the Temple of Hatshepsut still stand today.

DISCOVERY TIMELINE

C. 3100 BCE: Unification of Upper and Lower Egypt

C. 2780 BCE: King Djoser builds the first step pyramid.

C. 2686–2160 BCE: Old Kingdom

C. 2560 BCE: The Great Pyramid is built by King Khufu.

C. 2034–1650 BCE: Middle Kingdom

C. 1550–1069 BCE: New Kingdom

C. 1478–1458 BCE: Rule of Hatshepsut as pharaoh

30 BCE: Death of Cleopatra; Egypt becomes a Roman province.

GLOSSARY

afterlife (AF-tur-life)—the life that some people believe begins when a person dies

assassinate (us-SASS-uh-nate)—to murder a person who is well-known or important

CT scan (SEE-TEE SKAN)—a picture taken by a special X-ray machine to create a 3D image of a person's body

dynasty (DYE-nuh-stee)—succession of rulers from the same family; a powerful family or group of people whose members retain their power and influence through several generations

Egyptologist (ee-jip-TOL-uh-jist)—someone who studies Egypt

famine (FA-muhn)—a serious shortage of food resulting in widespread hunger and death

hieroglyph (HYE-ruh-glif)—a picture or symbol used in the ancient Egyptian system of writing

monument (MON-yuh-muhnt)—a large structure built in honor of a person or event

papyrus (puh-PYE-ruhss)—a tall water plant that grows in northern Africa and southern Europe; a material that is written on can be made from the stems of this plant.

regent (REE-jent)—a person appointed to rule in place of, or together with, another

X-rays (EKS-rays)—photographs of the inside of a person's body

LEARN MORE

Cruz, Jose. *Searching for Cleopatra's Tomb*. North Mankato, MN: Capstone Press, 2025.

Faust, Daniel R. *The Rise and Fall of Ancient Egypt*. Minneapolis: Bearport Publishing Company, 2025.

Britannica Kids: Pharaohs
kids.britannica.com/kids/article/pharaoh/400147

National Geographic Kids: Ancient Egypt
kids.nationalgeographic.com/history/article/ancient-egypt

INDEX

ABOUT THE AUTHOR

Carol Kim believes books and words have a magical ability to change the world, and she writes for children with the hope of spreading some of that magic. She is the author of the picture book biography, *King Sejong Invents an Alphabet* as well as more than three dozen fiction and nonfiction books for the educational market. Carol loves unearthing real-life stories and little-known facts to share with young readers. She lives in Austin, Texas with her family. Learn more at her website: CarolKimBooks.com.